Blue Sky Days to Come

Poems by Pam Pointer

First Serve Publishing

First Serve Publishing
30 Longhill Drive
Salisbury SP2 8TD

Blue Sky Days To Come
Copyright © Pam Pointer 2015
Design: Nicky Edwards

All rights reserved

No part of this book may be reproduced in any form by photocopying or any electronic or mechanical means, including information storage or retrieval systems, without permission in writing from both the copyright owner and the publisher of the book.

www.pampointer.co.uk
pampointer26@yahoo.co.uk

ISBN: 978-178456-264-9

First published 2015 by
FIRST SERVE PUBLISHING
An imprint of Upfront Publishing of Peterborough, England.

Contents

Spring's progression 5
A day of spring's emergence 6
Crushed 7
Honestly God 8
Welsh lamb 11
Bernard's beard 11
God is crying again 12
The merits of a cow 13
In bits – 1941 14
Arms 15
Badger 16
The Isle of Wight from Bournemouth Beach 17
Horse-chestnut's spring drama 17
Parlours 18
Shark 19
Cricket 1 – batsman 20
Cricket 2 – spectator 20
Cricket 3 – bowler 20
Penelope 1 – the bumblebee 21
Penelope 2 – my friend 21
The skyscraper dance 22
Bop for God 23
Donkey 23
Military camp 24
Pheasant 24
After the heatwave 25
Front seat upstairs 25
Last throes of summer 26
Eyesight 26
First day at school 27
Pig at Bramshaw 27
Jarrow march 28

One way traffick	29
Jarrow again?	30
Debt	31
In London wear black	32
Autumn commute home	32
Armistice at the Cenotaph	34
Poppies 2	35
Autumn tapestry	36
Slipping south	37
Dealing with the gap	38
Four-way man flu	39
Winter sunrise	40
Umbrellas' misfortune	41
Sanctuary	42
It is Christmas day	44
Just one snowflake	45
To such a world as this	46
Full moon	47
The Mousetrap	48
Too many	49
When Alzheimer's hits	50
International Space Station	51
A clutch of clichés	52
Joy comes in the morning	53
Out of a listless sky	54
Blue sky days to come	55

Spring's progression

In the gentle time of early Spring
translucent lime green beech leaves
filter sunlight tentatively
to the emerging life below
where primroses and violets,
delicate and dainty,
decorate the damp earth.

But before long
clouds of cow parsley
with legions of nettles
thrust wildly from the startled earth
in a frenzy of proliferation,
to assault and overwhelm
the brief presence of
bashful bluebells
who bow before their brash bold brothers.

As April and May's mad march moves on,
the canopy spreads
to obliterate the sky
and we welcome the green parasol
that provides shade from the noonday heat.
By June nature has calmed down
and we've grown used to the change
from brown, bleak, bareness
to the full colour palette of summer.

A day of spring's emergence

Early morning fog
smothers her brain
in a blanket of woolliness
and she can't settle...

She sits at the table,
gazes out of the window
at the dimmed circle of sun
burning slowly through
the sheet of cloudy gauze;

Heads of dancing daffodils
bob to the gentle music
of a lightening, brightening day
where shadows paint the grass
in dappled deeper shades;

Trees that drooped and dripped
cold tears of condensation early on
now lift bare branches and yearn
to burst into the song of new growth;

In the warming air of a now golden afternoon
bees burrow deep
into the recesses of yellow trumpets,
emerge to buzz and bustle here and there
with all the fizzy joy of Spring;

She sits on the bench outside the door
basking in that welcome
first warm sunshine of the year,
and dreams of more such days to come

when summer's song will trill
with the laughter of happy children
running, leaping,
delighting in outdoor freedom,
their fun made complete
by licking dripping ice cream cornets
and sipping home-made lemonade.

Crushed

Snail's slimy slither for survival,
silently repeated day after day,
ends abruptly
when a size nine boot
crushes her spiralled home.

Shell-shocked, she stops.
She knows this time
it is the end;
the crunch moment.

Slowly she shrivels
and with a last sob
succumbs
and surrenders the struggle.

The giant walks on
in his size nines
oblivious to what he's done.

Honestly God

Honestly, God,
you wouldn't believe
how dishonest we are.

Some of us
like to keep up appearances,
pretend we know it all,
have the monopoly on truth,
and say we do it your way
when we mean we do it our way.

Some of us
pretend that doubt is wrong
shouldn't or doesn't exist
that faith means complete confidence
all the time.

Some of us
well, me, really Lord,
think it's time for an honest chat
if you can take it.
So here goes: questions asked
with a wobbly heart
a weeping eye
and a yearning for truth.

Some of us
believe this is your world
so why do we pretend it's ours
and muck about
and chuck away
and duck responsibility
and tuck in
and wish better luck
on those who can't?

Some of us
say you're in control
but doubt it;
pretend to be stoical
but curse our suffering;
ponder and wonder
if you're even there at all.

Some of us
look at the stars
who pout and preen
enjoy being seen,
while we feel invisible,
insignificant nobodies
who question whether
you really rate us
like you say you do.

Some of us
see those other stars
that fight for sight in our
light-polluted lands,
trillions of sparkling dots
billions of light-years away
some already dead.

If all that's real
what are we that you care
for mere mortals,
fallible, gullible, laughable?

It's scary, Lord, being human,
and there are days when it
all seems pointless, purposeless
and exhausting,
but you know that.
You were homeless, a refugee,
lived in an occupied country,
were spat at, betrayed, and
murdered.

Thank God that you weathered it,
conquered it, and said it's OK,
all will be well.
I can be more real with you
than with any of my fellow-humans,
particularly those who think they've
got it all sorted and make me feel
I'm a lost cause.

One day my Prince will come
and we shall, for sure, live happily ever after,
the sorted and the muddled,
jumbled up together, at one with the One
who makes all things new.

Welsh lamb

Welsh lamb
blissful,
ignorant,
in mountain meadow,
lifts his head,
and turns a sweet face
to Spring sunshine;

All too fleeting
is this bleating bundle
of heart-beating life,
as, oblivious to fate,
he leaps in joyous bliss;

An all-too-brief life
ends
on a plate;
ah, bitter-sweet taste
this Welsh lamb.

Bernard's beard

When brother Bernard grew a beard,
his sisters firstly stood and peered
then leered and jeered
but never cheered,
they feared, alas, he'd gone quite weird.

God is crying again

God is crying again;
not just a single sob
nor a snuffling snivel,
but copious and prolonged
floods of tears.

Raining down from heaven,
drowning the earth with his sorrow;
tears of frustration,
disappointment,
and deep grief.

Here is the sadness of a father
observing his rebellious children
with love and continuous
unflinching devotion.

He sees them floundering
wringing their hands and wet clothes,
struggling through slippery mud
stumbling through deep waters
impotent and desperate
yet not seeking their father's help;
indeed, forgetting that he's there,
unacknowledged, ignored.

God is crying again.
He longs to intervene
but doesn't. Not yet.
Perhaps, one day,
those children will return to him.
He'll run to meet them
and the sunshine of his love
will suffuse them with light and warmth
and they will walk with him on dry land.

The merits of a cow

Let me tell you here and now
all the merits of a cow;
she can't give jewels or spin fine silk,
but think of all those pints of milk!
Then there's cheese and luscious butter
(hear those doctors fuss and mutter;)
lovely leather, cuts of meat;
Well done, cow, that's no mean feat.

In bits - 1941

An arm in the gutter,
its pair yards away;
a booted foot
with bloodied sock
legless
on a drain cover.

Body parts,
dozens of them,
torn from their source of life,
lay randomly
in rubbled streets.

A fireman retched
then got to work,
fetched bits into bags,
comforted a man
who screamed tearlessly
for his broken wife
so cruelly torn from him.

Not Iraq, nor Afghanistan,
no desert landscape;
not Vietnam nor Cambodia,
no napalm jungle scene;
not Syria, nor Egypt,
no Middle Eastern mess;
No, this was London,
blitzed to bits;
bits of buildings,
bits of bodies,
and a fireman's mind in bits.

Shell shock?
Post-traumatic stress syndrome?
The living nightmare
of a fireman in 1941.
He was no soldier,
he carried no firearms,
only a futile fire hose
in shaking fingers.

Just doing his bit
that turned him to bits,
but, unlike so many,
he lived,
sort of,
and told.

Arms

They're arm in arm till the call to arms means he's under arms and
she's at arm's length and up in arms and would give her right arm
to welcome him back with open arms;
but now he holds arms, presents arms,
bears arms, and has his arms full with
      harmful arms,
      lethal arms,
      deadly arms.
Fired up, others fire arms,
and he lays down his arms
for good.

Badger

He pads silently
through the woods at night,
his white stripe faintly visible,
a streak of subdued light.

His snout snuffles for food,
and for a few minutes
he has a cautious frolic
before he shuffles back
through the comparative safety
of his front door
to his home below.

Dawn breaks
and, above him,
humans tread his walks
and sigh
and speak of him
and sift their different points of view.

Friend or foe?
Fate or fortune?

Badgered to save badgers,
Badgered to slay them.

The Isle of Wight from Bournemouth Beach

The Isle of Wight has disappeared,
lost in mists of sea, sky, time.
Needles, now pointless,
lighthouse redundant,
coloured sands rubbed out.

All obliterated.

A silent shroud smothers the space
where island life once thrived.

But elegies for a premature death,
if not exaggerated,
are, it seems, erroneous,
for tomorrow's dawn,
in sparkling clear epiphany,
brings revelation:
The old things that had passed away;
have reappeared as new.

Horse-chestnut's spring drama

Taut sticky buds
in winter simplicity
give way to outrageously oversized leaves
and colossal candelabra
that break out in a burst
of extrovert extravagance.

Parlours

"Will you walk into my parlour?"
Said the farmer to the cow,
"It's time again for milking,
And you need to come right now."

The cow, alas, was grumpy,
"I would rather not today;
There must be other parlours
I could visit, if I may?"

"Well, which one takes your fancy?
We could try out one or two,
Er, how about a massage
Or a colourful tattoo?"

The cow, in rumination,
Felt that some were not for her,
Nails and cats and tanning,
All that varnish, paint and fur.

And then she had a brainwave
So did a little skip,
"I'd like to have an ice cream,
A luscious mint choc chip."

The farmer duly took her
To see how it was made,
She saw the milky mixture
And was suddenly dismayed.

Though she ate the tub of ice cream
And its smooth taste was like balm,
She knew, all of a sudden,
That her place was on the farm.

"Will you come into the parlour?"
Said the farmer to the cow,
"Why, yes! They need my milk, so
I'm coming in right now."

Shark

A shocking shark
devised a lark
to make his mark
around the ark,
so in the dark
he tried to bark;
his coarse remark
was heard on Sark.

Cricket 1 - batsman

At the Test
did his best
opened chest
hit with zest
then he messed;
guess the rest.

Cricket 2 - spectator

Got a ticket
for the cricket
watch them pick it
hit it, risk it,
flick it, nick it,
that's a wicket.

Cricket 3 - bowler

So to win
bring on spin;
aims for shin
hits a chin!
Hear the din
for his sin.

Penelope 1 - the bumblebee

Penelope, the bumblebee,
is full of glee and repartee,
her pedigree and jeu d'esprit
win devotees who come to tea.

Penelope 2 - my friend

My friend was named Penelope;
Such false, pretentious pedigree
caused ignorant catastrophe
and far too much hyperbole;
Confusion reigned when she was wee
and sadly shaped her destiny;
It's English! Such absurdity
of letters, etymology;
Pronunciation devotees
are puzzled and so disagree;
We surely need a referee
to deal with such diablerie,
for nothing helps Penelope
whose parents' importunity
spelled disaster, can't you see?
Her name, it rhymes with envelope,
Her parents called her Penelope.

The skyscraper dance
(with thanks to Lewis Carroll and The Lobster Quadrille)

"Shall we climb a little higher?" said the Gherkin to the Shard,
"There are others round about us who might threaten our back-
    yard.
See how eagerly the builders and their towers all advance!
They are waiting here in London to come and join our dance.
Will they, won't they, will they, won't they, will they join our
    dance?

You can really have no notion how delightful it could be
If they join us both still higher; what a view we all would see!"
But the Shard replied, "Too high, too high!" and he gave a look
    askance,
Said he thanked the Gherkin kindly but, please, no more to join the
    dance.
Would they, should they, would they, should they, would they join
    the dance?

"What matters it how high we go?" his piquant friend replied.
"There is another view, you know, to see it from their side.
The higher up we live and dwell, the more we'll all advance,
So don't be hard, beloved Shard, just give the rest a chance.
Will you, won't you, will you, won't you, let them join your dance?"

Bop for God

Come alive! Boogey, jive,
Jump and skip, swirl your hips,
Hop and bop, reel and squeal,
Rock 'n' roll, Living Doll,
Highland fling,
Laugh and sing,
Banish fear, go on, cheer!
Rid your doubts, move and shout!
Springsteen, Strauss, Shadows, House,
Beatles, Bach, Walton, Clarke,
Mix them all, have a ball!
Music fair, pleasure's there,
Sing and, dance, play and prance,
Praise and pray, make God's day.

Donkey

Soulful, docile and meek
he humbly hangs his head,
bears his cross with dignity,
and walks with measured tread
quietly through the Forest.

Military camp

Spiralled barbed wire
coils across the gate where,
in fatigues,
a soldier, gun poised,
keeps guard.

Enter if you dare;
some do.

Buzzards, kestrels,
swoop and soar;
indiscriminate gulls
lacking discretion,
peck and scratch,
screech and snatch
meagre rations
from pale grass,
ignoring guns
and tanks
and ranks of
battle-weary
fatigued soldiers.

Pheasant

It's never very pleasant
to see a car-struck pheasant
whose highway-crossing skill
is, sadly, not too brill.

After the heatwave

Cirrus clouds in
white wispy whirls,
of pale Paisley swirls
lie lazily
in the palest of blue skies,
hinting apologetically,
these reluctant heralds,
that rain is on its way.

Front seat upstairs

I wish they'd put in wipers on the top deck of the bus,
The windscreen's splattered over with dead flies and muck and
      dust,
The view from here is tainted coz I'm looking through a haze,
Oh how I wish they'd fix it; it would so enhance my gaze.
Alas, the weather's changing, the screen's peppered now with rain,
A monochrome mosaic fills the wretched window pane,
I long to put some blades in to swish the torrid glass
For future front-seat punters; clear views would be first class.

Last throes of summer

Flaxen threads in
straw-strewn lanes,
golden quilts of
hay-stacked fields,
bronzing leaves on
burdened trees,
clear blue skies of
chilling dawns,
signs of summer's
decline and
fall.

Eyesight

How strange it is that
I need specs to see
words on a page
just a few inches from my nose,
and other glasses to watch TV
just across the room,
and yet
in the clear blue dome
of a May morning sky
I see clearly
the half-sphere
of the dimpled creamy moon
hanging silently
in space
two hundred and thirty eight thousand,
eight hundred and fifty seven miles away,
reflecting the light
that dawns across the other side of the sky.
How strange it is...

First day at school

The first few falling leaves
of autumn drop in sympathy
with the first few falling tears
of a mother
on her child's first day at school.

Pig at Bramshaw

Punk pig
sports multiple nose-rings
and hoovers acorns.

Droopy ears scuff the ground,
hide lustrous-lashed eyes
and muffle snuffles as he
fusses and feasts, till
filled to satisfaction,
he straightens,
and moves to heave his bristly body
up and down a rough-barked oak.

Itching done
he flops heavily
onto his side,
closes those piggy eyes,
wrinkles punky nose,
snores,
and dreams
of tomorrow's Forest fun.

Jarrow march

Defeated
by a demolition job on
shipbuilding and morale,
feet, booted out and booted up,
walk south.

Nerves of steel,
wills of iron,
for a feat of endurance
that will not secure respite
from the harrowing hurt of
extreme poverty,
unemployment
and empty bellies.

They walk down
through coal and steam,
textiles and glass,
lace and leather,
past spas and markets,
cars and aeroplanes,
oscilloscopes, electronics,
gas appliances, furniture,
to the architectural superlatives
of the Marble, yes, marble Arch.

From North to South,
from poverty to the home of wealth,
from impotence to the seat of power,
From whence cometh their help?
Not from government, alas,
but from kindly souls along the way
who provide food and shelter,
offer listening ears,
understanding words,
and new boots.

One way traffick

Come, the man says,
I give you work
and thousands of rupees;
So I come,
I take the job
and wait
for thousands of rupees
that don't come
ever.
I work
twenty one hours
every day
on meagre rations
little sleep and
no money;
I've gone
from home to hell:
one way traffick.

Jarrow again?

Eight decades on.
Is there the will and energy
to march once more?
Or do history and despair
spawn apathy that languishes in
ghettos of neglect,
where the rejected and dejected
and too weary to fight for life?

Who will take up their call,
fight on their behalf?
City banks, food banks,
millionaires, paupers,
fat cats, alley cats?

Another pair of feet walks
with the downtrodden,
shines his face
on all his beloved beings,
whatever their state and status,
or lack of it.

God! Act through us all!
Sharpen our arrows of desire,
fire up our chariots,
will us to fight for justice,
to rebuild brokenness,
as we march in time with you.

Debt

Ends won't meet
haven't met for months

and for months
shame stopped her
from seeking advice

till desperation won
and she sought help
from a financial man

who disclosed his fees
when she'd disclosed her debts;

gut-wrenching fear
hollow-hearted despair

and the vortex
of downward spiralling
poverty
misery
and argument

circle savagely
on and on
for more months

world without end

In London wear black

In London
on the Tube
people wear black.

Black jackets
as if in deep mourning.

Deep underground
they stare blankly
fiddle with phones
yawn
and yawn again.

Black coats
black trousers
black bags
black boots

but a few
wear brown.

Autumn commute home

The moon hangs
pale and silent
in a late afternoon sky
over London;
out of reach of The Shard,
out of the sight of three men
on the 17.20 from Waterloo.

Their eyes are fixed
not on the glories
of this golden autumn evening
but on their tablets
and phones
and ipads and ipods,
whose glaring screens show
news, weather, games and messages.

Thumbs and fingers fiddle,
brows pucker,
and they miss the drama
of an ever-rising moon,
and the sinking sun
that brings a Midas touch
to bronzing trees
as London's random skyline
is left behind and southern shires beckon.

They miss the sun sink
beneath the western rim,
and miss the ascendancy
of that other orb
which now, bold and bright
against the darkened sky,
takes its turn of supremacy.

They miss it all,
this day/night progression of sky lights.

Armistice at the Cenotaph

Shadows of living soldiers,
grey-clad on grey tarmac,
double the numbers gathered
on this November morning
where falling autumn leaves,
gloriously golden,
drop silently to herald
The Glorious Dead.

The Glorious Dead,
remembered not as grey shadows
but in stark stones,
white and regimented,
and on village crosses
and in scarlet poppies
and in the bleeding hearts
of those who mourn them.

O God, our help in ages past
our hope for years to come,
Your will be done on earth
as it is in heaven.
Forgive us; we who send
these so young people to
fight and fall for freedom.
We will remember them.

Poppies 2

Swathed in waves of wheat
and meadow grasses,
scarlet poppies sway silently
in a shivering breeze.

A breeze that heralds
storm-clouded skies,
and in the dawning darkness
a cruel blood-spattered landscape.

In the ensuing quiet
a nervous peace soughs in.
And seeing it all,
God sighs and weeps
and waits.
All heaven waits.

And poppies shiver
to the rhythm of remembrance.

Autumn tapestry

The woods are flaming
with red, yellow
and bronze leaves

tumbling, twirling
in the wind
swirling into drifts

to be scuffed through
and thrown high
to fall in new patterns

with which no carpet weaver
could compete
on his clanking loom;

Here is God's
gleeful autumn spectacle
where rain-blackened bark

and sun-kissed golden leaves
sparkle, sing and show
the season's glory.

Slipping south

When
I began I
was tiny
and
helpless
dependent on
others for my needs
but gradually my horizons expanded
from a room
to a loving home
to the street and town
to the seaside and countryside
and eventually to far-flung corners
of the Earth, as I stretched my wings
soared up and out, enjoyed life to the full
until slowly but surely
my world shrank
my ageing body
slipped south
and now
I'm back
to where
I began
in one
room
where
I wait
helpless and dependent
and contemplate the end

Dealing with the gap

They fight
for justice
and fairness
and try to
plug the gap

between those who have
and those who have not

between those who are
down on their luck

and those who are
oblivious to it

between bailiffs
and bewildered

between debt collectors
and debt-ridden

between powerful
and powerless.

They skim the surface
in an effort
to help some
of the helpless

while others
sink lower
and drown
in desperation.

Four-way man flu

I'm
so ill
feel chill
take pill
stay still.

I'm
laid up
bunged up
het up
fed up.

I'm
in bed
nose bled
sore head
great dread.

I've
got bug
need drug
keep snug
'neath rug.

Winter sunrise

Cold earth slowly stirs,
reluctant to wake,
yet drawn to this new dawn
which, in the east,
with a soft-hued pearly glow
and gentle flush,
already hints at the promise
of a spectacle to come.

Beneath the horizon,
embedded behind frosted pale grass
and skeletal wintry trees,
the sun lingers longer,
while pale shades of primrose, lavender and pink
give way to startling gold, amethyst and ruby,
as God, with no constraints,
paints the lightening sky.

With what delight, joy, mirth,
he sweeps the sky with
bold strokes from his saturated palette;
He scales the heights, creates a fiery sight
as fun-filled fervour grips his brush with the sun.

The sky, now ablaze, holds the gaze
of wondering eyes
as the Creator of light,
in an ever-changing painting,
gives it his best golden touch
and raises the orb itself,
elevates it till, exalted and complete,
it dominates and dazzles all it shines upon.

Such glorious art!
Such work of imagination, skill and pleasure!
Reflecting his glory and beautiful to behold,
this awesome canvas
invigorates a waking world,
delights and inspires
its emergence from winter's night
to the adventure of a new day.

umbrellas' misfortune

It rained today, and how!
Howling wind
wound round legs
that legged it through the gale
to the cherished comfort of
fireside chairs, from which
tales of the storm were
regaled with relish.

But outside, perishing,
abandoned by erstwhile companions,
awkward broken spokes
poke out at rakish angles
from bins along the homeward route
and torn shreds of fabric
wave morosely,
speaking silently, reproachfully,
of their misfortune.

Sanctuary

Under cover of darkness
on a bitter winter's night
the metal-ringed handle
of a heavy, arched oak door
is turned, and they enter a covered space
where earth meets heaven,
where death meets life.

Flat stone-slabbed benches
border a short, flagged aisle;
and here, in the porch,
they find refuge from cold and rain
on bum-numbing beds that
provide mind-numbing rest
from weary ways.

By daybreak, bin-bagged belongings
are bundled beneath the bare beds,
and their owners are gone
till nightfall when, once more,
this chapel of ease
becomes a soothing sanctuary
where distress is dissipated,
sorrows drowned, suffering stifled,
and where losses of family, job, home,
health, dignity and worth
are temporarily sentenced to oblivion.

Here is respite from the bleak adversity of
a now luckless, lacklustre life.
Here, within these half-hallowed walls,
cigarette smoke, alcohol fumes
unwashed bodies and human waste, meet
incense, communion wine,
the body of Christ, and nourishment.

Jesus Christ!
You of the ignominious birth in a cowshed!
You, a homeless refugee!
You, who suffered...
and in this halfway house of yours,
you welcome those who are like you,
yet unlike you.
You understand their beleaguered state.
You offer
home for the homeless
help for the helpless
hope for the hopeless.

It is Christmas Day

It is Christmas Day in the doss house
And the cold bare walls a sight
With patches of mould all blackened
And the men in a dreadful plight
For with lined and sunken faces
In a long and hungry line
The vagrants sit dejected
With nothing on which to dine.

It is Christmas Day in the Jones' house
And the cold lounge walls are bright
With strips of paper streamers
And mocking fairy lights,
But with sad and careworn faces,
Too weak and tired to whine,
The children sit dejected
With nothing on which to dine.

The recession has hit them badly,
There's no work, no cash, no food,
They sit resigned and weary,
No joy, no festive mood.
The Government ignores them
And wishes they weren't there,
Just hoping other people
Will hear the cries and care.

It is Christmas Day in the stable
And the hay-strewn floor is bright,
A swaddled babe in a manger
Is illumined by strong starlight,
And for all those hungry people
Who span Earth's tired timeline,
He comes, this God, as man, and
Offers them bread and wine.

Just one snowflake

Tumbling silently
unique but not alone,
one snowflake
in the crowded sky
captivates my vision.

It twirls and twists,
a dull white speck
from laden leaden sky,
then brighter and whiter
as it flutters past my face.

Down, down, down
till it hits the warmer road
and vanishes.

To such a world as this

Rhythmic swaying oceans, dawn's bird symphony,
lively leaping lambs, butterfly ballet;
nature pulsates and proclaims Paradise
in dances of harmonious joy.
    To such a world as this
    a Saviour came.

From star-studded space,
over snow-iced mountains,
through bronzed beech woodland,
past rain-sprinkled rose buds,
to a wooden crib, in such a world as this,
he came.

But look closer, as he did,
at uncivil wars, at soul-destroying slavery,
and down into the drowning depths of depression;
see injustice, inequality, injury, illness, indignity,
and fast money fuelling fat cats,
while many, unable to choose, fast by fate.
    To such a world as this
    a Saviour came.

Control-compulsion masks a world that spins
beyond human control,
where man's best efforts to impress, reach out, relieve,
are flawed and finite;
where children cry, mothers mourn and fathers falter
for lost livelihoods, lost homes, lost limbs, lost lives.
    To such a world as this
    a Saviour came.

Still comes,
from Crib to Cross, to crowned Kingship,
to rescue and re-clothe his world
with beauty, joy and peace;
to bring light, liberty, laughter, life,
to restore Paradise.
    To such a world as this
    the Saviour comes.

Full moon

Strange solid orb of
rigid rock and dingy dust
- abandoned, bleak and barren

You shine
in meek magnificence
and gentle luminosity
on our bewildered Earth

Your silent circle
hangs,
unflawed in its fullness,
like finest porcelain
on the ebony dresser of the sky,
and gazes
with translucent serenity
and sympathy
on the dense solidity
of our dark night.

The Mousetrap

Agatha Christie
wrote a mystery
where unsure hosts
served eggs and toast
to several guests
resembling pests.

Lying low,
housebound by snow,
some were scared
and tempers flared;
they came to blows
as tension rose.

An awful cry
and someone died.
Who did this crime
in winter time...?
You know full well
that I won't tell.

Too many
(inspired by Thomas Hardy's Jude the Obscure)

Too many
ice bergs calving, polar bears starving,
rising oceans, lethal potions,
ivory poachers, phone call hoaxers,
black markets, child targets,
scared eyes crying, soldiers dying,
fatuous laws, slammed doors,
national debts, pampered pets,
strains of flu, points of view;

Too many
artics' loads, pot-holed roads,
traffic jams, reckless spams,
Twitter touts, litter louts,
graffiti walls, nuisance calls,
burgers, chips, fat tums, hips,
light pollution, revolution,
gabbling speakers, babbling squeakers,
powerful, shrill, men who kill;

Too many
down-trodden weak, with thin physique
who feebly yelp for needed help,
fratricide, matricide,
the tragedy of suicide.
How many
poor vulnerable
Little Father Times will walk and talk
and sigh and die
because we are too many?

When Alzheimer's hits

She sits
passively,
silent,
while others
chatter
and share
news and views.

They include her
as best they can,
speaking to her
with kindness
and compassion,
though no response
comes.

No words
No action
No wriggling
No giggling
Nothing

Except a smile

A smile that stays
and sometimes widens
and reaches her eyes.

This lovely lady
once communicated
in words that touched
the lives of thousands.

Wisdom,
practical help,
gentle humour,
all came from her lips
and from her pen.

God knows
how much she takes in now.

And what does she give out?
Just that beautiful smile
that speaks volumes.

International Space Station

In a star-sprinkled sky
the full moon stares,
startled by a special star
they call the International Space Station;
it whizzes soundlessly
at high speed,
filled with people who,
as they pass The Plough,
stare back at the moon
and down to the planet
they know as home.

A clutch of clichés

One day at a time, they say;
be in the moment;
just chill.

Oh, he feels the chill all right,
but it's not all right.

We understand, they say,
but however well-meaning their platitudes,
they don't.

Cheer up, it could be worse, they say,
And it is.

This black tunnel
(and don't remind him there's a light at the end)
goes on
and on.
His legs are leaden,
his brain numb.

He longs to soar,
to pierce the grey
and fly as free as a bird,
carefree instead of careworn.

Where there's life, there's hope, they say,
but in these dark, fog-heavy days,
there seems no hope.

And yet
he knows that, somewhere up there,
the sun - though now obliterated
by this smothering, breath-sapping
oppressive grey cloud of
seemingly impenetrable density -
is still there.

It waits
to pull away his fear and sorrow,
the anxious exhaustion,
the crushing emptiness,
to reveal light and warmth,
to infuse him to the core
and remind him that
after this oh so long and weary winter
summer will return.

Joy comes in the morning

Tears of night subside
as morning dawns
and creation wakes
to dance to the rhythm of day
on heather hillsides,
through whispering woods
and on shushing shingle shores.

Lord, in nature's movements
you hint at a new creation day,
when Paradise will be restored.
So today I wake, content
and at peace in your presence
and wait with hope
as you fill me with joy.

Out of a listless sky

Out of a listless sky
burdened with greyness
and the ominous threat of depression,
a thin strip of sunlight appears.
It is at the lowest point
on the eastern horizon ;
a golden gleam that backlights
shivering skeletal trees.
And then it's gone,
blanked out by overbearing cloud
that silently sneers
and snuffs the glint that dared
for one brief moment
to blink.
And yet,
that little glimpse
is enough for now,
a hint of hope,
of better days to come,
for the light, though hidden,
is always there
and can never
be extinguished.

Blue sky days to come

Hidden under a white blanket
and kissed surreptitiously
by a fleeting feeble sun,
aconites keep snug,
hardly move,
just whisper
to each other
about blue sky days to come
when they can emerge,
and lift their faces to
reflect the sun
and give joy
to waking workers
walking into town
as winter wanes
and Spring springs once more.